MW01074843

Shackled Again?

*From Slavery to Civil Rights: A Journey
Through Race Told Through The Stories
of Unsung Heroes*

SHACKLED AGAIN?

ISBN:978-1-4675-68203

by

Tony Watkins

Noir Notes Creative Services
Montgomery, Alabama

Dedication

This book is dedicated to my mother Ms. A.W. Salary
and "Ma'dear", my great grandmother Mary E. Russell
Watkins, who inspired me through her stories
to write this book

*On the cover is a photo of my great grandmother's
mother's aunt Martha Washington in 1911.*

Acknowledgements

"Shackled Again?" is a collection of conversations, observations and information I found on my journey to better understand race in this country.

This book would not have been possible without personal accounts of events, places and personalities, photographs, papers, oral histories and other materials provided to me by Joanne Bland, Rev. Frederick Douglas Reese, Afryia We-Kandodis, Pearlie Walker, the National Voting Rights Museum in Selma, Alabama, Sherry Sherrod DuPree, Sephia Shuttlesworth, Emory University and Tuskegee University archives, photographer Lloyd Wolf, and the Alabama Department of Archives and History.

I would also like to thank my editor Mona Davis for her professionalism and encouragement, and my family and friends who encouraged me to write this book.

I could not have done this without your support.

Contents

Shackled Again?

S hackles were a cruel tool used to restrain the movement of animals, prisoners or, for the purposes of this book, slaves. To give you an idea of how shackles functioned, they were round, iron metal bands joined by a forged link of chain.

Shackles were used on slaves mainly during transport, punishment or when transferring their ownership at the market.

These iron bonds came to represent what a life of captivity was for a slave: a fearful existence of poverty and cruelty, back-breaking work and broken family bonds. It was, in essence, a life devoid of any choice.

I marvel at the determination and sheer will it must have taken to endure such cruelties. Being so far removed from those atrocities today, it's very hard to imagine what it must have felt like to be shackled like that.

"Shackled Again?" explores the deep and lasting stain left by the institution of slavery on our country. It is a collection of stories, historic documents, photos and personal accounts that chronicle events and personalities from the Civil War to the Civil Rights Movement. It examines how far we have moved forward (or regressed) in regards to race and equality in our country.

This book asks the readers the important question "Are we shackled again?" Physically--- maybe not, but I think a compelling argument can be made that in many ways we still are. Shackles are no longer the chains we were forced to wear by a master that controlled every facet of life. Shackles evolved over time to Jim Crow, cheap labor, ghettos, employment discrimination, crime, broken families and generational poverty.

So are we shackled again? When I think about this, I am reminded of Thomas Jefferson's words in 1782 when he asserted:

"The whole commerce between master and slave is a perpetual exercise of the most unremitting despotism on the one part, and degrading submission on the other. Indeed I tremble for my country when I reflect that God is just; that his justice cannot sleep forever."

It is my hope that this book will awaken many of us out of complacency and will challenge us to break the shackles that hold our communities captive and prevent them from being everything they can be.

Chapter One

Ole Rosanna

A slave tied to a whipping post.

L ike many generations of African-American children in the South, the children in my family all grew up in close proximity to one another. We spent a lot of time on the front porch of my great-grandmother Mary E. Russell Watkins house. Ma'dear, as she was called, didn't let us hang around inside the house because she said she wanted her house to stay cool.

I remember the old smokehouse where she would hang the slaughtered hogs from the rafters. The boards in the smokehouse were soft because they were soaked with salt and grease. During the fall, the men would go on a hog killing, and I watched Ma'dear take those boards and cook them right into her soup. She said the salt and fat from the boards made the soup taste good.

The afternoons my cousins and I spent with Ma'dear on the front porch or gallery, as it was called, were special. She would sit in a chair with a wide-mouth bowl squeezed tightly between her knees as she shelled peas. We often helped her shell the peas and to pass the time she would tell us stories that had been told to her about our family history.

She loved to talk about her grandmother Rosanna Jefferson, who was born a slave in 1856 on Jefferson Plantation in South Carolina. Ma'dear described her as a tall, slim lady with thick, gray matted hair, high cheekbones, a flat-spread nose, and a small waist.

Grandma Rosanna was sold and brought to Alabama around age 10. She did not know what became of her mother and father. She never saw or heard from them again.

One of the worst conditions that enslaved people endured was to live under the constant threat of being sold. Even if their master wasn't overly cruel or treated them well, the slaves knew that a financial loss or another personal crisis could lead them to the auction block. Also, slaves were sometimes sold as a form of punishment, and although popular sentiment (as well as the economic self-interest of the owners) encouraged keeping mothers and children and sometimes fathers together, this was not always done. Immediate families were often separated. If they were kept together, they were almost always sold away from their extended

Mary E. Russell Watkins, "Ma'dear" age 94, taken November 2012

families. Grandparents, sisters, brothers, and cousins could all find themselves forcibly scattered, never to see each other again. [1]

Ma'dear said Grandma Rosanna and the other slaves were weighted down with 40 pounds of chains and many of the women cried as they were forced onto the wagons to be transported to Alabama.

Grandma Rosanna and the other slaves found themselves on a farm in rural Lowndes County, which at that time, was a complex isolated, close knit, and hierarchical slave society. She adjusted to life there, and soon gained a reputation for working from "can to can't."

Her duties included pulling weeds in the garden and feeding the livestock, sheep and hogs. In the evenings, she helped the adults pick cotton. According to Ma'dear, she and the other slaves had to pick a certain amount of cotton each day. If they did not, they would receive a severe whipping.

Life was very hard for Grandma Rosanna, but she learned how to weave yarn to make clothes — a skill she passed on to her daughter.

Rosanna liked to sing, as many slaves did, to pass the time and overcome the tedium of their work. Ma'dear said one slave would give a "corn-field holler" to start the song and the other slaves would join in singing. Grandma Rosanna's favorite song was "Swing Low, Sweet Chariot." It was a funeral song, yet it was fitting in many ways because many of the slaves longed for death because it was a chance to be free from their bondage.

I spent many weeks pouring through census documents, marriage certificates and other tax records and other public records in a vain effort to find out if Grandma Rosanna had any siblings. I learned that she had 10 children after slavery, the rest of the blanks were filled in by Ma'dear.

When I was about 10 years old, Ma'dear told me a story about Rosanna that I've never forgotten. To me, the story speaks to the cruelty Blacks endured both during and after slavery and how even after the slaves were freed; Blacks were still shackled by an oppressive social and political system that did nothing to protect them.

> *"When my grandmother was young, just about your age, maybe 7 years old, she liked to sit under a big oak tree and read the pictures, since she didn't know how to read. One day a white man, who was an old nigger trader, saw her reading. He became angry, snatched the book from her, dragged her from beneath the tree and began beating her. He made a small brush fire, and grabbed her by the arms and forced her hands into the fire. Rosanna was never the same after that. She lost the feeling in both hands which turned the same color as burnt coal."*

I remember crying as Ma'dear told me that story, but she admonished me not to be sad. "No one can burn your hands for trying to learn now. Remember good does not exist without evil. Promise me that you will keep going in school as far as you can."

I promised her that I would, and after a heartfelt prayer with my great-grandmother, I wiped the tears from my eyes and read to her the 23rd Psalms. After I'd finished she whispered to me, "make me proud" and gave me a warm kiss on the cheek.

My childhood is filled with memories of Ma' dear's stories, but it was an experience I had as an adult that made them all the more real to me.

It was April 2009, and Ma'dear sent me to clean the old mill shack on the property so we could put more hay inside for the cows. It was a blue kind of morning and the sun shone incredibly bright. The foliage had just changed colors and I was looking forward to being outside.

It's was roughly midday and I stood inside the old structure that sat on 40 acres of open field. This was not a run of the mill shack; it was actually a structure where slaves lived. The shack was over a century old and was constructed of plywood and two-by-fours.

It had a fireplace with a rack in the chimney and it was big enough to hold long logs. The shack had one window, two doors and a tin roof. The floor was rotten and broken up in the center, and part of the tin roof was bent backwards, which permitted the light from the sun to shine on that part of the floor.

I grabbed the pitchfork and began to break up the dirt. After several strokes I heard a loud clanking sound. I thought it was just an old, rusty drink can but as I dug further down into the soil, the sound grew louder.

The pitchfork struck a piece of metal, so I scooped around it to loosen the dirt beneath. As I cleared it away, I raised up the pitchfork and from one of its pointed teeth, a pair of iron shackles hung.

The old shack on my great grandmother's property where I discovered the shackles.

The shackles had eight hand-forged links that were hand twisted by a blacksmith. The first link on the right had been cut two-thirds through the metal. The shackles are believed to be over 150 years old.

Swing Low, Sweet Chariot,
Coming' fer to carry me home
I looked over Jordan an' what did I see,
Comin' fer to carry me home?
A band of angels comin' after me
Comin' fer to carry me home

The song "Swing Low, Sweet Chariot" always made her feel better. It was as if she knew there was a better place. She often said those old people could really sing. Below is Rosanna's headstone. She died on August 9, 1947 at the age of 98 in rural Alabama.

Now, my aim was not to conjure up an old relic from a painful past, and the magnitude of what I had just found wasn't lost on me by any means. The fork stuck inside the brace of slavery, and for a second, had brought it back to life.

Suddenly, I felt weak and exhausted and excited. Without any doubt, I could not fully grasp what had just been bestowed upon me. The five pound wrought iron shackles were at least 150 years old or more. They had been worn so much that the inner brace was smooth and the braces appeared to be stained. A historian told me those spots were blood stains from sores that mixed with the metal and changed the color.

The shackle had eight hand-forged links that were hand twisted by a blacksmith. The first link on the right had been cut two-thirds through the metal, and I could imagine someone trying in desperation to escape the shackles yet was dreadfully unsuccessful.

None of the braces or links were alike. The five-inch long key holder had a latch that had been hammered at the tip, but it was still in one piece.

The shackle survived as a painful reminder of the past as does slavery's painful legacy.

Tony Watkins **FOX ten**
Found slave shackles news

Interview with a reporter from FOX 10, where I talk about the shackles and their historical significance.

1794-1861

The link had been cut two-thirds through

Chapter Two

General Wilson and the Slave Who Saved Marengo Plantation

"Uncle Jeff, an ex-slave on Deer Plantation in Clairborne, Alabama, 1890-1899.

L ittle is known about Marengo Plantation and the slave that saved it from General James T. Wilson and his troops during the Civil War.

To fully understand the story, you have to understand the complex relationship between slaves and their masters. Though slavery took many forms, the underlying concept was always the same. Slaves were considered to be property — nothing more, nothing less— and this status was maintained by force. The social culture reinforced this belief, and though blacks and whites lived in close proximity to one another, the distinction was clearly understood by both races.

It would be too simplistic to say that all masters and slaves hated each other. Human beings who live and work together are bound to form relationships of some kind, and some masters and slaves genuinely cared for each other. But the caring was always tempered by the view that slaves were "not like us"… they may not have even been considered human in a sense. They were nothing but property. [2]

Life as a slave was brutally hard. The slave drivers, plantation overseers, and masters were responsible for discipline, and slaves were punished for not working fast enough, for being late getting to the fields, for defying authority, for running away, and for any number of other reasons.

The punishments took many forms, including whippings, torture, mutilation, imprisonment, and being sold away from the plantation. Sometimes slaves were murdered.

Slaves throughout the South lived under a set of laws called the Slave Codes. The codes varied slightly from state to state, but the basic idea was the same: the slaves were considered property, not people, and were treated as such. Slaves could not testify in court against a white person. They could not make contracts, leave the plantation without permission, strike a white person (even in self-defense), buy and sell goods, own firearms, assemble together without a white person being present, possess any anti-slavery literature, or visit the homes of whites or free blacks.

The killing of a slave was almost never regarded as murder, and the rape of slave women was treated as a form of trespassing.

In light of this culture, it was surprising to me to learn about the story of Marengo Plantation in Lowndes County and how a slave saved it from a Union Army.

Marengo Plantation evolved from a widely scattered small pioneer community into a thriving commercial center toward the later part of the 18th century. People flocked to the town for its new school, and because it was a popular trading spot for goods and merchandise that was shipped up the Alabama and Mobile rivers, it drew merchants and both black and white customers.

People would often travel by steamboat or horse and carriage to get to Marengo Plantation. They would spend the night at one of the two local taverns just so they could be among the first to arrive at the plantation the next day to purchase the best of the merchandise before it was shipped to Montgomery.

These were the days of "King Cotton" and since Lowndesboro was in the heart of the Black Belt and was so near to the Alabama River, much of the area grew and prospered. Just when Lowndesboro was at its peak, the Civil War began, and plantations all over the south feared raids by Union soldiers.

General Wilson's raiders, led by an Indian guide in full regalia, made their march from Selma to Montgomery and burned almost everything in sight.

There was no reason why Marengo Plantation wouldn't suffer the same fate, but it was saved by the most unlikely of persons — a slave.

Upon receiving the news that General Wilson's troops would be arriving in Marengo, Dr. Charles Edwin Reese, a local physician wrapped a slave in a white sheet and placed him in a barrel. He went into a nearby Union camp and convinced General Wilson that he should pass by the next town on his rampage, because it was suffering through a smallpox outbreak. In reality, the doctor

Union Army General James T. Wilson

was only treating the slave for a bad rash, but the ruse worked and Lowndesboro was spared as General Wilson moved on to raid Montgomery. [3]

General Wilson and his small band of raiders camped near Rosewood Estate and the Brown place which joined Rosewood estate on the north. In an account given by Mary Robinson Brown she stated:

> *"Only women, children, and very old men were left in town. There was no one at home but my mother and me and the servants. Squads of Yankees broke through the front gate and then divided into two groups: one group going to one side of the house and the other group to the other side so as to intercept anyone who might try to get away. They jumped off their horses and dashed through the house, breaking open trunks, drawers and closet doors, scattering the contents over the floors. It was rumored that my father had gold in the house, because he had removed his money from the bank and buried most of it. But fearful that the Yankees might burn the house or mistreat the occupants if they didn't find any money (as was their custom), he left a small amount of gold in a sack in the sideboard in the dining room. My mother and I had taken our seats on the back porch when we heard the Yankees approaching, and from that location had a view of the sideboard. I saw the solider when he found the gold. He turned to see if any of the soldiers were watching him, and it was then that he noticed me. With the bag of gold concealed inside his shirt he stalked out to the back porch and, for a few minutes, stood threateningly over me. I did not betray him. I wanted them to finish their search and leave." [4]*

General Wilson was in Lowndesboro when he got the message that Richmond had fallen. In haste he left Lowndesboro and marched to Montgomery to join the regiments that preceded him in the march.

Chapter Three

Confronting Power: Breaking Shackles Through Black Resistance

36

Hunting Slaves in Lancaster County

Though many blacks were resigned to live as slaves, there were brave men and women who yearned for and defended their freedom. They refused to be shackled and were willing to take freedom forcibly, if necessary. Such was the case with slaves in Lancaster County, Pennsylvania on September 11, 1851 during an event that came to be known as the "Battle of Christiana."

Christiana was a peaceful neighborhood near the border of Lancaster County and was home to several freedmen who live peaceably among the whites in the town. The conflict started when Maryland planter Edward Gorsuch went in search of his slaves Noah Buley, Nelson Ford, George Hammond and Joshua Hammond who fled his wheat plantation, Retreat Farm, in Baltimore on November 6, 1849.[5]

Just one year after his slaves had escaped Congress passed the Fugitive Slave Act of 1850. It made aiding fugitive slaves illegal, punishable by a potential six-month jail sentence and a $1,000 fine. Refusing to help or impeding the capture of a fugitive slave also became a federal offense. The law also denied fugitive slaves the right to a trial by jury. As a result, slave catchers began aggressively pursuing fugitives throughout the North, sometimes kidnapping free blacks to sell them into slavery in the South. [5]

On August 28, 1851, Gorsuch received the news he had spent two years waiting for. A letter from an informant placed at least three of his slaves in Lancaster County, Pennsylvania. Some 3,000 free blacks and fugitive slaves lived in Lancaster County, one of the easiest places in the nation for slaves to cross from slavery to freedom. Lancaster had a highly organized Underground Railroad, with some 50 permanent "stations" scattered across its countryside. [5]

There, two of Gorsuch's escaped slaves were living with a free black farmer named William Parker, near Christiana. Parker, too, had run away from Maryland in 1839, and ran a self-defense group to protect the local community of free blacks from slave catchers.

After obtaining warrants in Philadelphia on September 9, Gorsuch, his son Dickinson, Deputy Marshal Henry H. Kline, and several other men rode west for Christiana. Word of their arrival, however, preceded them, for the Philadelphia Vigilance Committee, run by William Still, sent Samuel Williams, a black man active in the Underground Railroad, to warn Parker and the fugitives of their imminent arrival. Early on September 11, 1851, Gorsuch and his party arrived at the home of William Parker.

Parker's wife Eliza blew a horn out of the window of their home to signal to the neighbors and members of the self-defense group. Some 50 to 100 free blacks armed with guns, pitchforks, corn cutters, axes and other weapons ran to the house to help. Among the first to arrive was Castner Hanway, a white miller and Parker's closest neighbor. Hanway attempted to calm the mob and warned Gorsuch and Kline to leave before things turned violent. Elijah Lewis, who was a friend of Parker as well, was deputized by Kline and ordered to help recapture the slaves, but they refused. This was in direct violation of the Fugitive Slave Act, which made helping fugitive slaves a serious federal offense. Instead, Lewis and Hanway advised the sheriff and Gorsuch's party to leave. [5]

Gorsuch refused to leave without his slaves and the fugitives refused to surrender. After a brief standoff, gunfire broke out and Gorsuch fell mortally wounded to the ground. As Dickinson ran to help his father, Parker's brother-in-law shot him. Kline and the other members of Gorsuch's party fled with the mob following in hot pursuit. Dickinson would recover from his wounds, but Edward Gorsuch died at Christiana.

 Conflicting versions of the riot at Christiana spread like wildfire, igniting passions throughout the country. Some claimed that Dickinson Gorsuch and several blacks had also been killed, and that the women had attacked Gorsuch before finishing him off with corn-cutters.

In the days that followed, several groups of white vigilantes terrorized blacks living in Lancaster County in search of those who participated in the riot. But it was too late. Parker's entire household

had fled to Canada, traveling through Rochester, New York, where Frederick Douglass helped them to obtain passage on a steamer to Toronto. [5]

Many whites around the country were outraged and demanded justice. A grand jury in Lancaster County indicted 38 black men on 117 counts of treason — the largest number of Americans ever charged with treason in the history of the United States — including Castner Hanway, whom Deputy Marshal Kline accused of leading the mob and refusing to aid, as required by the Fugitive Slave Act, in the recapture of the escaped slaves.

Hanway's 18-day trial, which began on November 24, 1851, resulted in the jury finding Hanway not guilty of treason. Parker and Gorsuch's former slaves had already escaped to Canada, so the courts in Lancaster could not force them to appear at trial. Because few witnesses would agree to testify, the grand jury dropped all of the charges against the men in custody. In the end, the state courts failed to indict anyone for any crimes associated with the Christiana riot. [5]

Welcome to the New South

Chapter Four

Miles and Miles of Drought: Emancipation Brings New Shackles

Photo credit: Emory University

Throughout the late 19th century racial tension grew through-out the United States. In the south, people blamed their financial problems on the newly freed slaves that lived around them. Lynchings were becoming a popular way of resolving some of the anger that whites had in relation to the free blacks. From 1882-1968, 4,743 lynchings occurred in the United States. Of these people that were lynched 3,446 were black.

The Reconstruction Period (1865-1877) after the Civil War was a confusing time both politically, socially and economically for everyone. The nation had been deeply divided over the issue of slavery and state's rights, and Reconstruction brought on new uncertainty.

The end of the Civil War and the abolition of slavery raised complicated issues and dilemmas for Americans during the Reconstruction. After the Confederacy was defeated, the southern states were devastated physically and economically. Their political infrastructures were no longer legitimate and millions of slaves were now legally free. The South was to be transformed into a *free labor* economy, and white plantation owners could no longer exploit slave labor to harvest their crops, meaning a devastating economic loss for landowners. [6]

In 1862, Abraham Lincoln appointed provisional military governors to re-establish governments in Southern states recaptured by the Union Army. Aware that the presidential plan omitted any provision for social or economic reconstruction -- or black civil rights -- the anti-slavery Congressmen in the Republican Party, known as the Radicals, criticized Lincoln's leniency. The Radicals wanted to make sure that newly freed blacks were protected and given their rights as Americans. After Lincoln's assassination in April 1865, President Andrew Johnson alienated Congress with his Reconstruction policy. He supported white supremacy in the South and favored pro-Union Southern political leaders who had aided the Confederacy once war had been declared. [7]

Several attempts were made to restore slavery, but President Johnson failed to control Congress which meant it had enough votes to override any veto Johnson tried to impose which was pro-slavery.

Congress passed the Reconstruction Acts of 1867 that divided the Confederate states (except for Tennessee, which had been re-admitted to the Union) into five military districts. Each state was required to accept the Thirteenth and Fourteenth Amendments to the Constitution, which granted freedom and political rights to blacks.

Each Southern state had to incorporate these requirements into their constitutions, and blacks were empowered with the vote on paper. Yet Congress failed to secure land for blacks or make provisions to protect voting rights for blacks. As a result, blacks were still controlled politically, socially and economically by whites. [7]

The Freedmen's Bureau was created to oversee matters related to blacks. They were authorized to administer the new laws and help blacks attain their economic, civil, educational, and political rights. The newly created state governments were generally Republican in character and were governed by political coalitions of blacks, Northerners who had migrated to the South (called "carpetbaggers" by Southern Democrats), and Southerners who allied with the blacks and carpetbaggers (referred to as "scalawags" by their opponents). This uneasy coalition of black and white Republicans passed significant civil rights legislation in many states. Courts were reorganized, judicial procedures improved, and public school systems were established. Segregation existed but it was flexible. But as blacks slowly progressed, white Southerners resented their achievements and their empowerment, even though they were in a political minority in every state but South Carolina.

Most whites rallied around the Democratic Party as the party of white supremacy. Between 1868 and 1871, terrorist organizations like the Ku Klux Klan, murdered blacks who tried to exercise their right to vote or receive an education, or any whites who supported them. The Klan, working with Democrats in several states, used fraud and violence to help whites regain control of their state governments. By the early 1870s, most Southern states had been "redeemed" -- as many white Southerners called it -- from Republican rule. By the time the last federal troops had been withdrawn in 1877, Reconstruction was all but over and the Democratic Party controlled the destiny of the South. [7] Out of this time of great change, several groups of blacks and whites emerged. The first group of whites were what I'll call the "Good Ole' Boys." They were staunchly opposed to equality for blacks. They believed the races should not intermix and deeply resented the growing political power of blacks. They disliked the federal government's intervention and sought to limit black people's ability to vote and participate in the political process. Good Ole' Boys advocated violence and other tactics to disenfranchise blacks and "keep them in their place."

The second group of whites are what I will call the "Status Quoers." Many were abolitionists who were opposed to slavery on moral or religious grounds and believed the newly freed blacks should be protected and given some rights as Americans. But they by no means believed in the equality of blacks. They believed in the separate but equal doctrine and were opposed to social integration of the races.

The third group of whites are what I'll call the "Egalitarians." They believed all human beings are created equally in God's sight—equal in fundamental worth and moral status. They believed equality applied to skin color and any other differences between individuals.

During Reconstruction, Southern blacks faced the same difficulty Northern blacks had confronted. Even though they were free, they were still surrounded by many hostile whites. One freedman, Houston Hartsfield Holloway, wrote, "For we colored people did not know how to be free and the white people did not know how to have a free colored person about them." [8]

The first group of blacks were what I call the "Radicals." They fled the South for the North with dreams of a better life and to secure their new freedom. Between 1877 -1881 somewhere between 40,000-70,000 blacks left the former slave states in protest against the loss of political rights and sought equality and opportunity in the West. Many in this group saw education as the most important pathway for blacks to elevate their station in life. One of the most famous proponents of this school of thought was W.E.B. Du Bois. In his essay "the Talented Tenth" he said,

> *"How then shall the leaders of a struggling people be trained and the hands of the risen few strengthened? There can be but one answer: The best and most capable of their youth must be schooled in the colleges and universities of the land. . . . All men cannot go to college but*

some men must; every isolated group or nation must have its yeast, must have for the talented few centers of training where men are not so mystified and befuddled by the hard and necessary toil of earning a living, as to have no aims higher than their bellies, and no God greater than Gold. This is true training, and thus in the beginning were the favored sons of the freedom trained. Out of the colleges of the North came, after the blood of war, Ware, Cravath, Chase, Andrews, Bumstead and Spence to build the foundations of knowledge and civilization in the black South. Where ought they to have begun to build? At the bottom, of course, quibbles the mole with his eyes in the earth. Aye! Truly at the bottom, at the very bottom; at the bottom of knowledge, down in the very depth of knowledge there where the roots of justice strike into the lowest soil of Truth. And so they did begin; they founded colleges, and up from the colleges shot normal schools, and out from the normal schools went teachers, and around the normal teachers clustered other teachers to teach the public schools; the college trained in Greek and Latin and mathematics, 2,000 men; and these men trained full 50,000 others in morals and manners, and they in turn taught thrift and the alphabet to nine millions of men who to-day hold $300,000,000 of property. It was a miracle—the most wonderful peace-battle of the 19th century, and yet today men smile at it, and in fine superiority tell us that it was all a strange mistake; that a proper way to found a system of education is first to gather the children and buy them spelling books and hoes; afterward men may look about for teachers, if haply they may find them; or again they would teach men Work, but as for Life—why, what has Work to do with Life, they ask vacantly. . . ."[10]

Du Bois' critics also labeled him an agitator because he strongly advocated for civil disobedience and black resistance to the status quo.

The second group of blacks were the "Conservatives." They

believed blacks should work within the segregated system to make gradual changes in their social and political condition. This group believed blacks should learn a trade and be gainfully employed in order to be successful.

The most vocal proponent of this idea was Booker. T. Washington. An educator and reformer, Washington was one of the most influential black leaders of his time (1856-1915). He preached a philosophy of self-help, racial solidarity and accommodation. He urged blacks to accept discrimination for the time being and concentrate on elevating themselves through hard work and material prosperity. He believed in education in the crafts, industrial and farming skills and the cultivation of the virtues of patience, enterprise and thrift. This, he said, would win the respect of whites and lead to African Americans being fully accepted as citizens and integrated into all strata of society. [11]

Before the Civil War, most southern states made it illegal to educate slaves, out of the fear that literate blacks would be harder to control. Despite those efforts, many slaves did learn to read and write and African Americans had built, funded, and maintained almost 500 small schools across the South. [11] During the post-Civil War Reconstruction era, the number of schools and the literacy rate for African Americans increased dramatically due to the creation of the Freedmen's Bureau, which Congress established to oversee relief efforts and black education; and the American Missionary Society, which funded teachers for black schools. But despite this progress, life for blacks was still very difficult.

Working class blacks found themselves at the bottom of the socioeconomic ladder and were relegated to work as domestics or laborers on the railroads, steamboats, sawmills, and farms for very low wages.

Violence also increased as white resentment grew in response to the beginnings of black political empowerment. Black codes were developed and the few political gains that were achieved during the Reconstruction era slowly faded as the South developed laws that oppressed blacks socially, politically and economically.

Convict Leasing in the South

Convict leasing in the United States began during the Reconstruction Period (1865–1877) after the end of the Civil War. Farmers and businessmen needed to find replacements for the labor force once their slaves had been freed. Some southern legislatures passed Black Codes, to restrict free movement of blacks and force them into employment with whites. If convicted of vagrancy, they could be imprisoned. States began to lease convict labor to the plantations and other facilities seeking labor, as the freedmen were trying to withdraw and work for themselves. This gave the states a new source of revenue during years when they were financially strapped, and lessees profited by the use of forced labor at below market rates. Essentially whites in the criminal justice system colluded with private planters and other business owners to entrap, convict and lease blacks as prison laborers.

"Strange Fruit"
Lynching During Reconstruction

Photo credit: Emory University

Terrorist groups like the Ku Klux Klan used intimidation and violence to control blacks and reverse many of the political achievements blacks made during the Reconstruction Period. Lynching was often used to punish blacks who attempted to be educated, to vote, or who broke social codes.

Chapter Five

Hanging Black Mothers: Consequences of Resistance

"Blessed are the meek, for they shall inherit the earth." Matthew 5:5

As a child, I can remember the stories I heard from older adults about black men who were kidnapped, beaten and lynched. I remember seeing the horrible images of black men hanging from ropes in trees, but it was really difficult to absorb the fact that women and children were also murdered in this way. The sheer brutality, fear and the public spectacle of lynching made it one of the most powerful symbols of segregation and white supremacy.

Blacks growing up in the South during the 18th and 19th centuries lived under the constant threat of violence. In the South, an estimated two or three blacks were lynched each week in the late 19th and early 20th centuries. In Mississippi alone, 500 blacks were lynched from the 1800s to 1955. Nationwide, the figure climbed to nearly 5,000. Lynching was a humiliating act of mob violence, but the image of an angry white mob stringing a black man up to a tree is only half the story. Lynching was an act of terror meant to spread fear among blacks and serve the broad social purpose of maintaining white supremacy in economics, politics, and society. [12]

Anytime whites felt threatened, lynching increased. For example, though many blacks were hung during and after slavery, lynching increased during Reconstruction when viable black towns sprang up across the South and blacks began to make political and economic gains by registering to vote, establishing businesses and holding public office. Many landowners and poor whites felt threatened by the rise in black prominence and foremost on the minds of many was the irrational fear that black men were sexual predators that wanted integration in order to be with white women. [12]

Lynchings were often public events. They were advertised in newspapers and drew large crowds of white families with children. Photos of the victims, with exuberant white observers posed next to them, were taken for distribution in newspapers or on postcards. Body parts, including genitalia, were sometimes distributed to spectators or put on public display.

Blacks could be lynched for petty crimes like theft, but the biggest "crime" of all was to be accused of looking at or associating with a white woman. Many blacks were also murdered for refusing to back down from a fight with someone white or for being outspoken. Most victims of lynching were political activists, labor organizers or black men and women who violated white expectations of black deference and were deemed "uppity" or "insolent." Though most victims were black men, women were by no means exempt. [12]

"Bless the Lawd, the Yankee's Have Come" The Story of Amy Spain

---

Amy Spain was a 17-year old slave girl that was hanged in March 1865 just days before receiving her freedom. It is a reminder of just how unwilling those who had power were to relinquish it, and that the struggle for freedom often involved death, even for children.

Amy Spain was owned by Major A.C. Spain, a prominent local lawyer in Darlington, South Carolina who was considered a war hero during the invasion of Mexico in the early 1800s.

Union Army Gen. William T. Sherman's march through South Carolina began in early January 1865. By March 9, his troops had passed out of the state into North Carolina, leaving behind a path of destruction 100 miles wide and extending the entire length of the state. In view of the destruction of property, casualties to the Confederate and Union armies and the population at large was relatively light. About 1,000 people were killed and about 200 of those deaths in the Carolinas were civilians. [13]

As one could image, tensions were very high during Sherman's occupation of Darlington, but to many black slaves, it signaled that freedom was near. Amy Spain, unable to restrain her emotions at the news of the Union Army's nearby presence, clasped her hands and exclaimed, "Bless the Lord the Yankees have come!" The long night of darkness which had bound her in slavery was about to break away, and it was impossible to repress her joy. Yet, the simple act of expressing joy for her coming freedom was enough to seal her fate. [14]

There are several conflicting versions of what happened next to Amy Spain. According to an account in the September 30, 1865 edition of *Harpers Weekly*, Amy thought immediate liberation had come and she and others began taking household goods and clothing from their masters in preparation to leave. But by that time, Sherman's troops were already preparing to leave Darlington to liberate Florence, a large prisoner of war camp. Unbeknownst to the black slaves, Confederate troops were already returning to Darlington to restore order. Anger over the Union threat made Amy and the other slaves targets. She and others were promptly arrested. But Amy drew most of the whites' rage because of her outspoken declaration of freedom.

Major Spain accused Amy of stealing sheets, pillow cases, a large Brussels carpet, flour, sugar and lard. He also accused her of cursing at his children.

The article read:

> *"She was seized and hung to a*
> *Sycamore tree standing in front of the*
> *courthouse, underneath which stood*
> *the block from which was monthly*
> *exhibited the slave chattels that were*
> *struck down by the auctioneer's ham-*
> *mer to the highest bidder.*
> *Amy Spain heroically heard her sen-*
> *tence, and from her prison bars de-*
> *clared she was prepared to die. She*
> *defied her persecutors; and as she*
> *ascended the scaffold declared she*
> *was going to a place where she would*
> *receive a crown of glory. She was*
> *rudely interrupted by an oath from*
> *one of her executioners. To the eternal*
> *disgrace of Darlington her execution*
> *was acquiesced in and witnessed by*

most of the citizens of the town. Amy was launched into eternity, and the "Southern gentlemen" of Darlington had fully established their bravery by making war upon a defenseless African woman. She sleeps quietly, with others of her race, near the beautiful village.

No memorial marks her grave, but after ages will remember this martyr of liberty. Her persecutors will pass away and will be forgotten, but Amy Spain's name is now hallowed among the Africans who, emancipated and free, dare with the starry folds of the flag of the free floating over them, speak her name with holy reverence."[14]

The Lynching of Laura Nelson

When I was a child , I remember old black folks down in the country would warn the young boys that "standing up to white folks could get you killed."

Though I was aware of the social divide between blacks and whites, I never had the same frame of reference that they did. I didn't realize how easy it was for blacks to be accused of a crime, tried and murdered with very little or no evidence for minor infractions.

The story of Laura and Lawrence Nelson, a mother and son in Oklahoma, illustrates this point.

Laura and her 14-year-old son Lawrence were lynched after Lawrence was accused of shooting a deputy who was searching their family's cabin for stolen meat.

According to a 1911 newspaper account, Laura Nelson made a futile attempt to save her son's life by confessing that she shot the deputy, even though there was evidence that cleared her.

Laura Nelson and her son Lawrence Nelson lived in the town of Okemah, Oklahoma., shown above. According to the Oklahoma Historical Society, there were 147 recorded lynchings in Oklahoma between 1885 and 1930. Until 1907, most of the victims were white cattle rustlers or highwaymen, but after Oklahoma gained statehood in 1907 with a constitution that promoted racial segregation (Jim Crow laws), most of the victims were black. In all, 77 were white, 50 black, 14 American Indian, 5 unknown and 1 Chinese. Below, Laura Nelson and her son Lawrence Hanged from a bridge across the North Canadian River.

The boy's father also pled guilty to stealing cattle in order to save his son. He was taken to jail.

> *"Forty men rode into Okemah at night and entered the sheriff's office unimpeded (the door was usually locked). The jailer, a man named Payne, lied that the two prisoners had been moved somewhere else, but when a revolver was "pressed into his temple," he led the mob down a hall to the cell where Lawrence Nelson was sleeping. Payne unlocked the cell, and they took the frightened boy, "fourteen and yellow and ignorant," and "stifled and gagged" him."* [15]

> *"Next they went up to the female jail, a cage in the courthouse, and took the woman out. She was "very small of stature, very black, about 35 years old, and vicious." Mother and son were hauled by wagon six miles west of town to a new steel bridge crossing the Canadian River "in a negro settlement," where they were "gagged with tow sacks" and hung from the bridge. "The rope was half inch hemp, and the loops were made in the regular hangman's knot. The woman's arms were swinging at her side, untied, while about 20 feet away swung the boy with his clothes partly torn off and his hands tied with a saddle string. The only marks on either body were those made by the ropes upon the necks. Gently swaying in the wind, the ghastly spectacle was discovered by a Negro boy taking his cow to water. Hundreds of people from Okemah and the western part of the country went to view the scene."* [15]

Mary Turner's Story

In May of 1918, Hampton Smith, a 31-year-old white plantation owner in Brooks County, Georgia, was shot and killed by Sydney Johnson, one of his black workers. Hampton Smith was known for abusing his workers to the point that few people in the area would work for him. To solve his labor shortage, Smith turned to the convict leasing system of the day and found a ready labor pool. He would bail people out of jail who had been arrested for petty offenses. They would then work off their debt to him on his plantation. Nineteen year old Sydney Johnson, arrested for "rolling dice" and fined $30 dollars, was one such person. [16]

After a few days of work on Smith's plantation, and shortly after being beaten by Smith for not working while he was sick, Sydney Johnson shot and killed Hampton Smith.

Angered by the killing, a mob of white vigilantes went on a manhunt for Johnson and any others they suspected might have been involved. For more than a week, the mob killed 13 blacks. Of those killed was 28-year-old Mary Turner.

Mary Turner, who was eight months pregnant at the time, was outraged because her husband had been among the 13 black men killed during the mob violence. She publicly objected to her husband's murder and vowed to swear out warrants for those who were responsible. [16]

Those "unwise remarks," as the area papers put it, enraged locals. Consequently, Mary Turner fled for her life only to be caught and taken to a place called Folsom's Bridge near the county line. To punish her, the mob tied Mary Turner by her ankles, hung her upside down from a tree, poured gasoline on her, and burned her. One member of the mob then cut her stomach open and her unborn child was reportedly stomped on and crushed. Later that night she and her baby were buried 10 feet away from where they were murdered. The makeshift grave was marked with only a "whiskey bottle" with a "cigar" stuffed in its neck. [16]

Three days after the murder of Mary Turner and her baby, three more bodies were found in the area. Sydney Johnson was killed in a shoot out with police on South Troup Street in Valdosta, Georgia. Once killed, the crowd of more than 700 people cut off his genitals and threw them into the street. A rope was then tied to his neck and he was dragged to Campground Church in Morven, Georgia, 16 miles away. There, what remained of his body was burned. During these chain of events, it was reported that more than 500 black people fled Lowndes and Brooks counties in fear for their lives. [16]

Maggie and Alma Howze's Story

The story of Maggie and Alma Howze is as troubling as Mary Turner's because it demonstrates that blacks were easy targets for mob violence and false accusations, even where there was little or no evidence to prove any wrongdoing.

Maggie and Alma Howze along with others were accused of the murder of Dr. E.L. Johnston in December 1918. A white mob lynched Andrew Clark, age 15; Major Clark, age 20; Maggie Howze, age 20; and Alma Howze, age 16; from a bridge near Shutaba, a town in Mississippi.

The local press described Johnston as being a wealthy dentist, but he did not have an established business in the true sense of the word. He sought patients by riding his buggy throughout the community offering his services to the public at large in Alabama. Unable to make a living for himself and his wife and child as a traveling dentist, he returned to Mississippi to work on his father's land near Shabuta.

During his travels he developed an intimate relationship with Maggie Howze, a black woman who he asked to live with him. He also

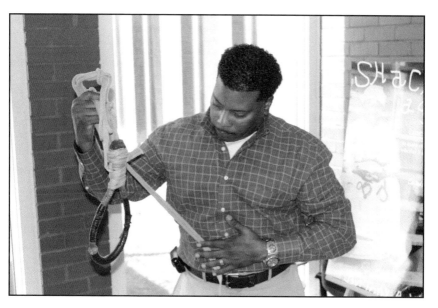

This noose, found in the Tuskegee University Archives, is similar to those used in lynchings.

asked that she bring her sister Alma Howze. Both women became pregnant by Johnston. [17]

Three black laborers worked on Johnston's plantation, two of whom were brothers, Major and Andrew Clark. Major tried to court Maggie, but Johnston was violently opposed to her trying to create a world of her own that did not include him. Johnston threatened Clark and soon afterward, Johnston turned up dead. Major Clark, his brother Andrew, and the Howze sisters immediately fell under suspicion. [17] They were arrested and thrown in jail despite the fact that Johnston's own parents felt that neither the Clark brothers or the Howze sisters had anything to do with their son's death. They believed, due to his business dealings, that an irate white man had killed their son, knowing that the blame might fall on his black workers.

Yet, to extract a confession from Major Clark, the authorities placed his testicles between the "jaws of a vise" and slowly closed it until Clark admitted that he killed Johnston. White community members took the four blacks out of jail, placed them in an automobile, and drove them to the lynching site.

Eighteen other cars, carrying members of the mob, followed close behind. Some of the men shut down the local power and the town was dark. Ropes were placed around the necks of the black men with the ends tied to the girder of the bridge.

According to published accounts of the event, Maggie Howze cried, "I ain't guilty of killing the doctor and you oughtn't to kill me." Someone took a monkey wrench and struck her in the mouth, knocking her teeth out. She was also hit across the head with the same instrument, cutting a long gash in which the side of a person's hand could be placed." While the three other blacks were killed instantly, Maggie Howze, who was four months pregnant, managed to grab the side of the bridge to break her fall. She did this twice before she died and the mob joked about how difficult it was to kill that "big Jersey woman." No one stepped forward to claim the bodies. No one held funeral services for the victims. [17]

The black community demanded that the whites cut the victims down and bury them. Wanting to prevent more unrest, the whites placed them in unmarked graves.

Alma Howze was on the verge of giving birth when she was killed. One witness account claimed that at her "burial on the second day following, the movements of her unborn child could be detected." [17]

Chapter Six

Remembering Rosewood

The home of James Wright, a white merchant who hid many black women and children in his home and in a well on his property during the Rosewood Massacre. Wright along with William and John Bryce, helped many escape Rosewood on a train owned by the Bryce brothers.

Almost 90 years ago, a small African-American community was nearly wiped out of existence. Racial violence, denial, and the deep pain and fear experienced by those who survived the massacre in Rosewood Florida in 1923 had all but erased the little known town from memory. It wasn't until the 1980s that ruins from the town were uncovered. That discovery sparked interest in the Rosewood story. An apology by the state of Florida, a major Hollywood movie, websites and books chronicling the event, and the oral histories of the survivors and their descendents have all contributed to make sure Rosewood and those who died there will never be forgotten.

"It All Began with A Lie"

Rosewood was established around 1845 in Levy County, Florida, which is fewer than 10 miles from the Gulf of Mexico. The town got its name from the beautiful red cedar trees that grew in the area. Local industry centered on timber and the town flourished due to the pencil mills, turpentine mills and a sawmill in nearby Sumner. The town served as a train depot for the Florida Railroad in 1870, but it was never incorporated officially as a town.

By 1890, the cedar in the area had been depleted. Most of the white families moved to Sumner, three miles west of Rosewood and worked at a new sawmill established by Cummer and Sons. By 1900 Rosewood had a black majority of citizens. The Goins and Carrier families were its leading black families. The Goins owned a turpentine mill and the Carriers had a sizable logging business. From most accounts Rosewood was a thriving, peaceful community that had always maintained harmonious relations with neighboring white communities.

That all changed on the morning of January 1, 1923 when Fannie Coleman Taylor of Sumner, Florida claimed that she had been attacked by a black man. According to reports, she was not seriously injured, but she allegedly remained unconscious for several hours due to the shock of the attack. Sarah Carrier, a black woman from Rosewood who did the laundry for Fannie Taylor, and other neighbors claimed that the man who attacked Fannie Taylor was actually her white lover. She had made the claim in an effort to conceal the beating she'd received by her boyfriend from her husband.

Yet, Taylor was readily believed. No one ever questioned her version of the story because for a black man to touch a white woman was an unpardonable sin, and retribution would be swift. Taylor's lie instigated a week of violence and terror on the citizens of Rosewood that resulted in the complete destruction of the town and the brutal murders of eight people. [20]

A telegraph sent to Gainesville, Florida by Fannie Taylor's husband, James Taylor, solicited the support of the Ku Klux Klan. Several of the black domestics who worked in white homes overheard telephone conversations calling on whites from other towns to come to Rosewood to help find Fannie Taylor's black attacker. According to reports, anywhere from 400-500 Klansmen came to Sumner looking for a suspect. Suspicion fell on Jesse Hunter, a black man who had allegedly escaped from a chain gang. But no proof of the escape was ever provided.

The mob descended on Rosewood because in their minds, they believed the black citizens were hiding Jesse Hunter. They captured, tortured and lynched a black man named Sam Carter, a local blacksmith, who they believed helped Jesse Hunter escape. They also seized Aaron Carrier, a relative of Carter, from his home as he slept. The mob yanked him out of bed, tied a rope around his neck and the back of a car and dragged him from Rosewood to Sumner. They tortured him until he lost consciousness.

Fear and panic gripped the citizens of Rosewood. Many began fleeing into the nearby swamps for protection. In an account given by one of the oldest living Rosewood survivors, Mary Hall Daniels, who was just three years old at the time, she described to interviewers Ryan Morini and Sherry Sherrod DuPree the terror she and others in the Rosewood community felt as they fled.

> *"Well the only (ones) was out there was my mother*
> *and five of us children. Because I had two sisters*
> *was living and my twin sister's name was Martha.*

She had died as a baby. So they ran to the woods. So everybody got out to the woods with the children and Mama starts counting the children; one was missing. And the missing person was me because I was the youngest and I was three years old at that time. She left me in the bed, she took my brother Charlie 'cause he always been kinda delicate..... And she was too scared to go back to the house to look for me, to get me. Now I don't know who went back to get me.. now that I never knew. But somebody went back to the house and got me out of the bed. And brought me, carried to the woods where my mother was. And we all stayed out there in the woods and my momma she could look from the woods out there and she could see the big flame of fire and smoke and everything, where everything was burned down. All the homes, all of the Black Americans' homes was burnt down and everything in it and everything we had was burnt up. And we had nothing but what we had on in the woods and I mean that was the gown or whatever I was sleeping in when they took me out of the bed and carried me where my mother was. So we stayed out there. So I don't know who was making the round for bringing us food or whatever they was doing...." [21]

Sarah Carrier

Sylvester Carrier

71

Sherry Sherrod DuPree
"Preserving the Rosewood Legacy"

Author, retired professor and historian Sherry Sherrod DuPree, Ed.S, first began working with the descendents and remaining survivors of the Rosewood tragedy during the late 1980s.

She agreed to help them by conducting research to support legal claims by family members for restitution from the state of Florida. At the time, many denied Rosewood's existence. Some even claimed that the massacre never happened.

DuPree and other investigators researched thousands of documents including insurance records, tax filings and other public documents. She also interviewed survivors and their family members to substantiate what really happened in Rosewood.

As a result of her research and efforts by others, the survivors and descendents of Rosewood were ultimately rewarded $2 million in compensation in 1994 for the state of Florida's failure to protect the citizens of Rosewood.

DuPree remains close to the Rosewood families and still works to preserve the Rosewood legacy through her service on numerous historical committees, and as a board member for the Rosewood Heritage Foundation. The prolific author is also a Smithsonian Institute Fellow, Library of Congress Ambassador, and director of the United Nations Educational Scientific and Cultural Organization's Transatlantic Slave Trade. Florida Center.

Sherry S. DuPree, left, with Alzada Harrell and Rosewood survivor Mary Hall Daniels. Daniels is believed to be the oldest living Rosewood survivor.

On the night of January 2, the mob returned to Rosewood and surrounded the Carrier house. But this time, they were met by a group of armed black men and friends from neighboring areas led by Sylvester Carrier. A gun battle ensued and after several hours, many members of the mob were shot or lay wounded in Carrier's mother Sarah's yard. Sarah Carrier had been killed earlier when the mob fired into her home, as she tried to hide young children.

The mob retreated and many of the black citizens of Rosewood who had been hiding in the woods or who had barricaded themselves in the Carrier home fled with the help of Sheriff Bob Walker who helped secure their escape by train. Over the next few days, remnants of the enraged mob returned to loot the homes in Rosewood before burning them to the ground. They also murdered any of the few remaining blacks who were either too old or too ill to escape. [20]

On February 12, 1923 a special grand jury was convened to investigate the massacre. After hearing the testimony of 25 white and eight black witnesses, the jurors reported that they could find no evidence on which to base any indictments. No one was ever criminally held responsible for the murders that took place in Rosewood. Defeated, the black residents of Rosewood left never to return. Many escaped to other cities. Many changed their names. For decades many never spoke of the atrocities that happen there.

It wasn't until May 4, 1994 — 70 years later— that the Florida Legislature publicly apologized to the remaining survivors and their descendents for the state's failure to protect the citizens of Rosewood. The Legislature passed the Rosewood Bill and through it agreed to compensate the remaining survivors and their descendants $2 million through a special fund. [22]

Ten years later Governor Jeb Bush dedicated a historic marker in Rosewood on May 4, 2004, in memory of the Rosewood citizens. [23]

Chapter Seven

"Sick and Tired of Being Sick and Tired": Breaking Shackles Through Political Empowerment

Sit-ins were an integral part of the nonviolent strategy of civil disobedience, ultimately leading to the passage of the 1964 Civil Rights Act. It was a method, largely utilized by students, where participants would sit at a lunch counter until they were served. If they were taunted, they did not respond; if they were hit, they did not retaliate, and they oftentimes dressed in their Sunday best. By August 1961, more than 3,000 students across the country were arrested. [30a]

V iolence, economic disparity, separate but equal facilities, voter suppression and Jim Crow proved to be effective shackles, but African Americans still challenged the system.

There was little justice due to the social, economic and political power structure and the hardness of men's hearts. Slavery's dark legacy extended well beyond the brutal working conditions in the cotton or tobacco fields or the pain inflicted by the cracking of the whip.

It, instead, evolved and grew into a legal, socioeconomic system that supported the belief that all blacks were inferior through segregation, strict social codes, and violence which was protected by the law. Breaking the shackles of slavery and ultimately Jim Crow would have to come through political empowerment and challenging America's attitudes regarding race.

If the 1950s and early 1960s were the decades for righteous idealism and hope for a swift conclusion to the civil rights movement, then 1966 was the year of dislocation and disarray. Fearing for their very survival, many African American men, women and children joined the nonviolent protest movement. They were simply "sick and tired" of the way things were.

There were many courageous individuals who took on that yoke of nonviolent resistance and placed it squarely on their shoulders. Some are well-known and others have been largely overlooked by history, though their roles were no less important. I want to share with you the stories of those unsung heroes I believe made an impact on the movement.

Fannie Lou Hamer

Fannie Lou Townsend Hamer was born on October 6, 1917 in Montgomery County, Mississippi. The granddaughter of slaves, she came from a long line of sharecroppers. She was also the last of 20 children born to Jim and Lou Ella Townsend.

At the age of six she worked alongside her family members in the fields picking cotton; and by the time she was 13 she could pick between 200 to 300 pounds of cotton.

Life was hard and she often dreamed of a better life for herself and her family. She wanted desperately to escape the crippling poverty and segregation that was common in Mississippi and often prayed that someday she would be able to make a difference.

In 1962, her prayers were answered. She began attending Student Nonviolent Coordinating Committee (SNCC) and Southern Christian Leadership Conference (SCLC) meetings. SNCC members were teens and young adults who defied segregation throughout the South by staging sit-ins and testing Jim Crow at "white-only" lunch counters, public accommodations and transportation, and by attempting to register to vote.

Though Hamer was in her 40s, she was eager to participate in SNCC activities. She became its field secretary and gathered names on petitions to obtain federal commodities for poor black families. She also taught classes for SCLC and heavily campaigned for voter rights in Mississippi in the face of overwhelming violence.

At sit-ins, which began in Mississippi in May 1963, participants were sprayed with paint and had pepper thrown in their eyes. Students who protested at the lunch counters after the bombing of NAACP field director Medgar Evers' home were beaten, and the kidnapping and murder of civil rights workers Michael Schwerner, Andrew Goodman, and James Chaney drew national outrage. Historian Charles Payne once said Mississippi had the highest rate of lynchings recorded with 539 between the end of Reconstruction and the early 1960s.

Fannie Lou Hamer testifies at the Democratic Convention about the violence blacks experienced in Mississippi for attempting to register to vote. Above left, Fannie Lou Hamer leads a group of demonstrators in song during the "March Against Fear" in Mississippi. The march was started by James Meredith, the first African-American to integrate the University of Mississippi. Photo Credit: Jim Peppler Archives

In 1963, after being charged with disorderly conduct for defying a restaurant's "whites only" policy, Hamer was beaten so badly in jail that she was permanently disabled.

In 1964, Hamer helped found the Mississippi Freedom Democratic Party, which was established in opposition to her state's all-white delegation to the Democratic convention. In her testimony at the 1964 convention, she described the brutality blacks faced for trying to vote and brought the civil rights struggle in Mississippi to the attention of the entire nation. [24]

> *"Mr. Chairman, and to the Credentials Committee, my name is Mrs. Fannie Lou Hamer, and I live at 626 East Lafayette Street, Ruleville, Mississippi, Sunflower County, the home of Senator James O. Eastland, and Senator Stennis.*
>
> *It was the 31st of August in 1962 that eighteen of us traveled twenty-six miles to the county courthouse in Indianola to try to register to become first-class citizens. We was met in Indianola by policemen, Highway Patrolmen, and they only allowed two of us in to take the literacy test at the time. After we had taken this test and started back to Ruleville, we was held up by the City Police and the State Highway Patrolmen and carried back to Indianola where the bus driver was charged that day with driving a bus the wrong color.*
>
> *After we paid the fine among us, we continued on to Ruleville, and Reverend Jeff Sunny carried me four miles in the rural area where I had worked as a timekeeper and sharecropper for eighteen years. I was met there by my children, who told me the plantation owner was angry because I had gone down -- tried to register.*

After they told me, my husband came, and said the plantation owner was raising Cain because I had tried to register. And before he quit talking the plantation owner came and said, "Fannie Lou, do you know -- did Pap tell you what I said?"

And I said, "Yes, sir." He said, "Well I mean that."

Said, "If you don't go down and withdraw your registration, you will have to leave." Said, "Then if you go down and withdraw," said, "you still might have to go because we're not ready for that in Mississippi."

And I addressed him and told him and said, "I didn't try to register for you. I tried to register for myself."

I had to leave that same night. On the 10th of September 1962, sixteen bullets was fired into the home of Mr. and Mrs. Robert Tucker for me. That same night two girls were shot in Ruleville, Mississippi. Also, Mr. Joe McDonald's house was shot in.

And June the 9th, 1963, I had attended a voter registration workshop; was returning back to Mississippi. Ten of us was traveling by the Continental Trailways bus. When we got to Winona, Mississippi, which is Montgomery County, four of the people got off to use the washroom, and two of the people -- to use the restaurant -- two of the people wanted to use the washroom.

The four people that had gone in to use the restaurant was ordered out. During this time I was on the bus. But when I looked through the window and saw they had rushed out I got off of the bus to see what had happened. And one of the ladies said, "It was a State Highway Patrolman and a Chief of Police ordered us out."

I got back on the bus and one of the persons had used the washroom got back on the bus, too.

As soon as I was seated on the bus, I saw when they began to get the five people in a highway patrolman's car. I stepped off of the bus to see what was happening and somebody screamed from the car that the five workers was in and said, "Get that one there." And when I went to get in the car, when the man told me I was under arrest, he kicked me.

I was carried to the county jail and put in the booking room. They left some of the people in the booking room and began to place us in cells. I was placed in a cell with a young woman called Miss Ivesta Simpson. After I was placed in the cell I began to hear sounds of licks and screams. I could hear the sounds of licks and horrible screams. And I could hear somebody say, "Can you say, 'yes, sir,' nigger? Can you say 'yes, sir'?"

And they would say other horrible names.

She would say, "Yes, I can say 'yes, sir.'"

"So, well, say it."

She said, "I don't know you well enough."

They beat her, I don't know how long. And after a while she began to pray, and asked God to have mercy on those people. And it wasn't too long before three white men came to my cell. One of these men was a State Highway Patrol-

man and he asked me where I was from. And I told him Ruleville. He said, "We are going to check this." And they left my cell and it wasn't too long before they came back. He said, "You are from Ruleville all right," and he used a curse word. And he said, "We're going to make you wish you was dead."

I was carried out of that cell into another cell where they had two Negro prisoners. The State Highway Patrolmen ordered the first Negro to take the blackjack. The first Negro prisoner ordered me, by orders from the State Highway Patrolman, to lay down on a bunk bed on my face. And I laid on my face, the first Negro began to beat me.

And I was beat by the first Negro until he was exhausted. I was holding my hands behind me at that time on my left side, because I suffered from polio when I was six years old.

After the first Negro had beat until he was exhausted, the State Highway Patrolman ordered the second Negro to take the blackjack.

The second Negro began to beat and I began to work my feet, and the State Highway Patrolman ordered the first Negro who had beat me to sit on my feet -- to keep me from working my feet. I began to scream and one white man got up and began to beat me in my head and tell me to hush.

One white man -- my dress had worked up high -- he walked over and pulled my dress -- I pulled my dress down and he pulled my dress back up.

I was in jail when Medgar Evers was murdered.

All of this is on account of we wanted to register,

to become first-class citizens. And if the Free-
dom Democratic Party is not seated now, I ques-
tion America. Is this America, the land of the
free and the home of the brave, where we have
to sleep with our telephones off of the hooks
because our lives be threatened daily, because
we want to live as decent human beings, in
America?

Thank you. [24]

From 1968 to 1971, Hamer was a member of the Democratic National Committee for Mississippi. Her 1970 lawsuit, *Hamer vs. Sunflower County*, demanded school desegregation.

She ran unsuccessfully for the Mississippi State Senate in 1971, but won a delegate seat to the Democratic National Convention of 1972.

She also lectured extensively, and was known for a signature line she often used, "I'm sick and tired of being sick and tired." She was known as a powerful speaker, and her singing voice lent another powerful element to civil rights meetings.

Fannie Lou Hamer brought a Head Start program to her local community with the help of the National Council of Negro Women, and helped found the National Women's Political Caucus in 1971, speaking for inclusion of racial issues in the feminist agenda.

In 1972 the Mississippi House of Representatives passed a resolution honoring her national and state activism, passing 116 to 0. In addition, she was a member of the board of trustees of the Martin Luther King Center for Nonviolent Social Change from 1974 to 1977.

Suffering from breast cancer, diabetes, and heart problems, Fannie Lou Hamer died in Mississippi in 1977. She had published *To Praise Our Bridges: An Autobiography* in 1967. June Jordan published a biography of Fannie Lou Hamer in 1972, and Kay Mills published *This Little Light of Mine: the Life of Fannie Lou Hamer* in 1993.[24]

Fred Shuttlesworth

In many ways, Rev. Fred Shuttlesworth was a lot like Fannie Lou Hamer—fearless and unsung. He was the soul of the civil rights movement and the designated leader of the movement in Birmingham, Alabama. He may have lacked Martin Luther King's eloquence, name recognition and ability to lead the masses, but he was honest and straightforward. He was a leader in his own right and spoke truth to power even if it ruffled feathers among his more famous contemporaries. Shuttlesworth was a man who did what he felt was right, lived on his own terms, and refused to back down. Though he didn't crave the national spotlight, he demanded respect. He was a community leader whose actions in Birmingham — a city that earned the dubious nickname "Bombingham" for its violence—transformed him into a national leader.

Born in Mount Meigs, Alabama, Shuttlesworth was Membership Chairman of the Greater Birmingham, Alabama chapter of the NAACP. The state of Alabama formally outlawed the civil rights organization from operating within the state in 1956, so in response, he and Ed Gardner established the Alabama Christian Movement for Human Rights (ACMHR).

The ACMHR raised almost all of its funds from mass meetings. It used both litigation and direct action to pursue its goals. When the authorities ignored ACMHR'S demand that the city hire black police officers, the organization sued. Similarly, when the United States Supreme Court ruled in December 1956 that bus segregation in Montgomery, Alabama, was unconstitutional, Shuttlesworth announced that the ACMHR would challenge segregation laws in Birmingham on December 26, 1956.[25]

Shuttlesworth survived many attempts on his life. When he and his wife Ruby attempted to enroll their children in a previously all-white public school in Birmingham in 1957, a mob including Klansmen, who were awaiting their arrival, brutally attacked them. One of the men involved was Bobby Frank Cherry, who was later identified as one of the 16th Street Baptist Church bombers.

The mob beat him with chains and brass knuckles in the street. His wife was also stabbed in the hip. Recognizing that the back door of the car was standing open, Shuttlesworth struggled to make his way back to the car. But he couldn't get to it because members of the mob were positioned near the door swinging chains to hit him. When the chains became entangled it allowed him the chance to dive into the back seat. Rev. J.S. Phifer, an injured Ruby Shuttlesworth and the three children were in the car. They helped to pull Shuttlesworth in and Rev. Phifer drove them to the hospital.[30]

On Christmas night in 1956, suspected Klansman placed 16 sticks of dynamite beneath his bedroom window. Though the house was severely damaged, Shuttlesworth escaped unharmed. A police officer, who was believed to belong to the Klan, told him as he came out of his home, "If I were you I'd get out of town as quick as I could." Shuttlesworth told him to tell the Klan that he was not leaving and, "I wasn't saved to run."

In 1958 Shuttlesworth survived another attempt on his life. A church member standing guard at his home saw a bomb and quickly moved it to the street before it detonated.

As pastor of Bethel Baptist Church from 1953 to 1961, he used the building as a meeting place for ACMHR. In retaliation for his activities, his church was bombed three times. One would think it would be difficult to hold fast to the nonviolent philosophy of social change in the face of such violence. Yet Shuttlesworth embraced that philosophy, even though his own personality was combative, headstrong and sometimes blunt-spoken to the point that he frequently antagonized his colleagues in the movement, as well as his opponents.[25]

He was not shy about asking Dr. King to take a more active role in leading the fight against segregation, and warned him that history would not look kindly on those who gave "flowery speeches" but did not act on them. He alienated some members of his congrega-

Shuttlesworth, seated right, with Freedom Riders on a trip to Mississippi during Freedom Summer.

tion by devoting as much time as he did to the civil rights movement, at the expense of weddings, funerals, and other ordinary church functions. As a result, in 1961 Shuttlesworth moved to Cincinnati, Ohio to take up the pastorate of the Revelation Baptist Church. He remained intensely involved in the Birmingham struggle after moving to Cincinnati, and frequently returned to help lead demonstrations.[25]

Shuttlesworth was arrested five times for his participation in the 1961 Freedom Rides; but never sat-in at segregated lunch counters or rode the busses.[30] He originally warned organizers that Alabama was extremely volatile when he was consulted before the Freedom Rides began. Shuttlesworth noted that he respected the courage of the activists proposing the rides but felt other actions could be taken to accelerate the civil rights movement that would be less dangerous. However, the planners of the rides were undeterred and decided to continue preparing.[26]

Shuttlesworth worked with the Congress of Racial Equality (C.O.R.E.) to organize the rides and became engaged with ensuring the success of the rides, especially during their time in Alabama. Rev. Wyatt T. Walker, who was executive director of the SCLC at the time, contacted Shuttlesworth once the plan for the rides was in place. He asked Shuttlesworth to be responsible for the Freedom Riders once they reached Alabama.

Shuttlesworth mobilized members of ACMHR to assist the riders. After the Greyhound bus was bombed in Anniston, Alabama on Mother's Day 1961, Shuttlesworth and his longtime friend and bodyguard, Colonel Stone Johnson, organized a nine-car caravan that went to Anniston to bring the Freedom Riders safely to Birmingham.[30]

James Reeb was a young white man who sustained serious head injuries during the attack. Shuttlesworth escorted him to the hospital once they returned to Birmingham. He gave him a dime to call him once he was released. He told him not to leave the hospital without calling him first because he feared that the Klan in Birmingham might try to finish him off. Once the hospital released Reeb, he contacted Shuttlesworth, who along with Colonel Johnson picked him up. On the way back, the car was pulled over by the police. When the officers saw Shuttlesworth inside, they radioed back to headquarters. The person on the other end of the line exclaimed, "Damn!" and told the officers to let them go. Had Shuttlesworth not been in the car, Reeb most likely would have been killed.[30]

Shuttlesworth took in the Freedom Riders at the Bethel Baptist Church and its parsonage, allowing them to recuperate after the violence that had occurred earlier in the day. The violence in Anniston and Birmingham almost led to a quick end to the Freedom Rides, however the actions of supporters like Shuttlesworth gave James Farmer, the leader of C.O.R.E., who had originally organized the Freedom Rides, and other activists the courage to press forward.

U.S. Attorney General Bobby Kennedy gave Shuttlesworth his personal phone number in case the Freedom Riders needed federal support. On one occasion when Shuttlesworth attempted to ride to bus, Kennedy phoned him and asked, "Reverend, must you ride the bus into Mississippi with the young people? God has not been to Mississippi in a very long time." Shuttlesworth answered, "That's why I must go. You see Mr. Attorney General, I must go and I must take God because he hadn't been there in quite a while."[30]

Shuttlesworth was also pivotal in launching the "Project C" campaign. The "C" stood for confrontation. The SCLC, which he cofounded with King and other prominent ministers, began a series of public, mass demonstrations to desegregate public accommodations in Birmingham. He and the others wanted business owners to feel the economic impact of segregation through boycotts and demonstrations. He hoped it would force them to integrate.

One of the 1963 demonstrations resulted in Shuttlesworth being convicted of parading without a permit from the City Commission.

On appeals the case reached the U.S. Supreme Court. In the 1969 decision of Shuttlesworth vs. Birmingham, the Supreme Court reversed Shuttlesworth's conviction. They determined that the parade permit was denied not to control traffic, as the state contended, but to censor ideas.[27]

In 1963 Shuttlesworth was set on provoking a crisis that would force the authorities and business leaders to recalculate the cost of segregation. He was helped immeasurably by Eugene "Bull" Connor, the Commissioner of Public Safety and most powerful public official in Birmingham. Connor frequently used Klan groups to heighten violence against blacks in the city. Even as the business class was beginning to see the end of segregation, Connor was determined to maintain it. While Connor's direct police tactics intimidated black citizens of Birmingham, they also created a split between Connor and the business leaders. They resented both the damage Connor was doing to Birmingham's image around the world and his high-handed attitude toward them.[26]

Shuttlesworth and Dr. Martin Luther King answer reporters' questions at a news conference in Birmingham, Alabama.

Shuttlesworth with his wife Sephira at a book signing event in Birmingham, Alabama.

Similarly, while Connor may have benefited politically in the short run from Shuttlesworth's determined provocations; that also fit Shuttlesworth's long-term plans. The televised images of Connor directing handlers of police dogs to attack unarmed demonstrators and firefighters' use of water hoses to knock down children had a profound effect on American citizens' view of the civil rights struggle, as well as people around the world.

Shuttlesworth's activities were not limited to Birmingham. In 1964 he traveled to St. Augustine, Florida (which he often cited as the place where the civil rights struggle met with the most violent resistance), taking part in marches and widely publicized beach wade-ins that greatly impacted the successful passage of the land-mark Civil Rights Act of 1964. Thus, he was a key figure in the Birmingham campaign that led to the initiation of the law, and the St. Augustine campaign that finally brought it into being.[28]

In 1965 he was also active in Selma, Alabama, and the march from Selma to Montgomery that led to the passage of the Voting Rights

Act of 1965. In later years he took part in commemorative activities in Selma at the time of the anniversary of the famous march, and he returned to St. Augustine in 2004 to take part in a celebration of the 40th anniversary of the civil rights movement there.[28]

During his lifetime, Shuttlesworth held the distinction of having more cases heard before the U.S. Supreme court than any other American, most notably *Sullivan vs. New York Times Co.*, the landmark case that established the legal precedent for libel and defamation. He called himself a lawyer without a portfolio because he spent a great amount of time studying the law looking for ways to bring about the changes he was seeking.[30]

Shuttlesworth's life after the movement was just a fruitful and rich. He founded the "Shuttlesworth Housing Foundation" in 1988 to assist families who might otherwise be unable to buy a home.

In 2001, he was presented with the Presidential Citizens Medal by President Bill Clinton, and in July 2008, the Birmingham Airport Authority approved renaming the city airport in his honor. On October 27, 2008, the airport's name was officially changed to Birmingham-Shuttlesworth International Airport.

On October 5, 2011, Shuttlesworth died at the age of 89 in Birmingham. The City of Birmingham announced that it intended to include Shuttlesworth's burial site on the Civil Rights History Trail. By order of Alabama Governor Robert Bentley, flags on state government buildings were lowered to half-staff until Shuttlesworth's interment.[29]

Chapter Eight

Stories from Selma: Personal
Reflections On the Movement
From Those Who Lived Through It

The Edmund Pettus Bridge in Selma, Alabama.

Selma, Alabama has a unique place in history because it was the site of perhaps one of the most pivotal events in the civil rights movement. On Sunday, March 7, 1965 — "Bloody Sunday" — a group of 600 demonstrators gathered at the foot of the Edmund Pettus Bridge in Selma to make the 54-mile march from Selma to the state capitol in Montgomery in support of voter rights.

By order of Alabama Governor George Wallace, sheriffs' deputies, 65 state troopers and a group of angry white civilians stood in firm opposition to the group of unarmed protesters led by SNCC leaders John Lewis and Hosea Williams. The marchers were beaten back across the bridge by law enforcement wielding tear gas, dogs, and Billy clubs. Some marchers were even trampled on by horses.

Television media coverage of the vicious attack on the marchers, provoked sympathy from across the nation and globe, giving the movement support and opening the eyes of the world to the violence perpetrated against blacks for simply trying to vote.

Public outcry and a strong desire in the movement's leadership ranks called for a second march, which would be held on March 9, 1965. This time, it would be led by Dr. Martin L. King.

Only the Southern Conference Leadership Conference (SCLC) was told about the second march in advance, which caused confusion and drew complaints from many, who were willing to travel long distances and risk their lives to participate in the march.

This march would include primarily religious leaders. It would be symbolic and would not be a full march to Montgomery; only to the foot of the Edmund Pettus Bridge.

In the wake of the violence that accompanied the first attempt, Federal District Judge Frank M. Johnson refused to grant permission for a march from Selma to Montgomery. To comply with Johnson's directive, Dr. King led about 2,500 marchers to foot of the bridge, then turned the marchers back around toward Selma. SCLC was careful not to violate Johnson's order since he was one of a few

Southern judges that was viewed as being fair and sympathetic to the movement.

Dr. King's action was widely denounced by both supporters and detractors. Many within the movement felt he should have defied the court order. Segregationists opposed to voting rights march wanted all the activity stopped, and that very night, three white ministers were attacked. One was killed by a white supremacist.

For the third march, SCLC again attempted to gain a court order that would prohibit any interference by law enforcement or others. This time, Judge Johnson granted an order of protection and on March 21 more than 3,000 marchers walked across the Edmund Pettus Bridge to the state capitol in Montgomery.

Protected by Alabama National Guard troops and federal marshals, by the time the marchers arrived in Montgomery, their numbers had grown to more than 25,000. The march had a significant impact on the passage of the Voting Rights Act of 1964, which was signed by President Lyndon just five months after the historic event.

Through the Eyes of A Child:

Joanne Bland's Story

"Growing up, I lived the pain and frustration of segregation. I experienced what it was like to be denied services and not be able to do the things I wanted to do just because of the color of my skin.

My mother Lundie Blackmon died in the hallway of the local hospital in Selma because she needed blood and the hospital didn't have "colored" blood. The blood had to be ordered from Birmingham, which was an hour away by bus. By the time my father got to the bus station to pick up the blood it was too late. My mother and the unborn child she was carrying had died.

My grandmother Sylvia Johnson left Detroit and came home to Alabama to bury my mother and take care of me and my three sisters and brother. She just couldn't understand how little things had

97

changed in Selma after 35 years. She called it the "Mason Dixie Mentality."

The loss of my mother and conditions in Selma made me believe that all bad things happen in the South. In my eyes, there wasn't anything good in Selma either. Like a lot of cities, Selma had a "Black section", where most blacks worked, went to school, worshipped and shopped. Everything you needed, for the most part, was located in "your section." When you ventured out of the section, you might encounter trouble.

My opinions began to change when my grandmother introduced me to a woman named Amelia Boynton and her husband Sam. The couple formed the Dallas County Voting League in the 1930s. The purpose of the League was to improve conditions for the black community in Selma through political action. They recognized that by registering people to vote and by electing representatives who had the best interest of the black community to office, things could change. Mrs. Boynton soon began taking me to League meetings.

I was of the generation where children were "seen and not heard." Me and the other youth had to sit quietly while the adults strategized.

My grandmother and I often went downtown and passed by Carter's Drug Store. Carter's had a lunch counter and I would look through the windows and stare longingly at the counter at the white children who were eating there. I saw them spinning around on the stools licking ice cream or drinking milkshakes from the beautiful glasses. I always wanted to sit in the high stool chairs and would imagine myself swinging my legs and twirling around the counter. I couldn't understand why I couldn't sit at the counter, even though my grandmother explained it to me many times that colored children could not sit at the lunch counter.

One day, my grandmother was talking to her friend in front of the store. I watched the children at the lunch counter and listened as my grandmother talked. She noticed me watching and she leaned over her shoulder and pointed at the window. "When we get our freedom, you'll be able to do that, too!" I smiled and in my heart I believe I became a freedom fighter that day.

When I was a little older, I began attending organizing meetings at First Baptist Church with my oldest sister Lynda. The non-violence resistance philosophy was hard to accept at that age. After all, in my neighborhood, if someone hit you on the cheek, you didn't turn the other one. If you didn't hit them back, they would be hitting you all day long and your head would be bopping back and forth.

But as I became more involved in the movement, I slowly began to understand that violence in any form is wrong.

By age 11, I was marching in protest movements. I remember what it felt like to kneel and pray on the front steps of the Dallas County Courthouse. Even though I was not old enough to register to vote, I still liked being a part of the action. We were taught to ask God to "lift the hearts of those evil men who would not let our parents vote."

But that routine got old quick. The sheriff began putting the pro-testers in jail. We were put in cells that were suppose to hold one or two people, but instead, me and about 40 others were jammed into the cells all at one time. If you were lucky enough to get a cell with a bed, you couldn't sit there long because the guards took the mattress.

The toilet was in the middle of the cell— that's where you didn't want to be. As far as the food went, the guard would take pride in bringing the protesters a plate of big rock (dry unwashed beans) in the morning for breakfast. And if you thought you were not going to eat it, by that third day you would push that rock aside and hope you didn't identify what you were crunching on.

There were a lot of things done in an effort to break our spirits while we were in jail. Once we were released, we went home, took a hot bath, ate a good meal, and returned to the courthouse to con-tinue protesting. By the time I was 11 years old I had already been to jail 13 times.

In December 1964, the Dallas County Voting League wrote a letter to Dr. Martin Luther King inviting him to speak in Selma in honor of the January 1 anniversary of the Emancipation Proclamation. Dr. King accepted the invitation and said in his speech that Selma, Alabama would be the battleground for voting rights in the United States. He was right.

Things heated up even more in Selma after that speech. Dr. King brought in his lieutenants and stationed them in the surrounding counties. There were marches all around Selma and Dr. King sent Rev. James Orange to Marion, Ala., which is in Perry County, to organize the children.

About 600 young protesters marched to the courthouse in support of voter rights, and all 600 were arrested. Around 3 p.m., a state trooper came into the area of the jail where Rev. Orange was and brought a rope that was tied into a noose. The state trooper threw it over the bars of that cell so that the noose hung in Rev. Orange's face all day. He did it to intimidate Rev. Orange, who knew full well that they were capable of carrying out such a threat. Eventually, the sheriff released the youth, but he kept Rev. Orange in custody.

Meanwhile, there was a mass meeting being held at Zion United Methodist Church that was approximately two blocks from the jail. The children ran into the church and disrupted the meeting. They told the minister, "You have to do something, now. They're going to kill him."

The people inside the church ran over to the jail and marched around it all night in hopes that their mere presence would save Rev. Orange's life. He was eventually released, but many of the adults were later attacked and brutally beaten by the law enforcement officers.

At that time, a young man named Jimmie Lee Jackson ran from the church to help his 82-year-old grandfather who he saw was being beaten by a state trooper.

Jimmie Lee pulled at the trooper and begged him not to hit his grandfather. He told him to just take him to jail if he had done something wrong, but don't beat an old man. Jimmie Lee's mother also saw the trooper beating her father too, so she ran over to help. This angered the trooper who drew back his Billy club to hit her. Jimmie Lee tried to shield his mother by putting up his hands and was shot by the officer.

He died eight days later at Good Samaritan Hospital in Selma. After his death, the Dallas County Voting League decided to march from Selma to Montgomery to protest Jimmie Lee's death and to demand the right to vote.

Jimmie Lee Jackson's death really affected us. We were afraid, but we believed in what we were doing and we were committed to it. On March 7, Bloody Sunday, John Lewis and Hosea Williams led a group of marchers down Broad Street to the Edmund Pettus Bridge. We were met by a wall of policemen.

John Lewis asked the policeman to let us pass. The policeman said "there won't be any march between Selma and Montgomery, and you have three minutes to disburse and go back to your children."

The next thing I heard was a gunshot. People began to scream and run, but it was too late. The police officers began moving in from both sides and in the front and back. We were trapped. There was nowhere to go. They began beating people old, young, black and white, male and female. Blood was everywhere. Many were so injured that they were believed to be dead, but you could not stop to help them. The troopers began shooting tear gas inside the crowd. It burned my eyes and got into my lungs making it hard to breath. You couldn't see what was in front of you, and often times you would run back into the same people you are running from . I remember it seemed like an eternity.

Even now, 47 years later, I can still hear those screams. The screams were coming from fear: being afraid of the horses, of being beaten and kicked, of having bones broken, of being trampled, and of being killed.

The last thing I remember that day was finding my sister who'd been beaten so severely that she suffered a head wound that required over 20 stitches. Yet, the following Tuesday, we went back to the bridge, held hands and marched with Dr. King and Rev. Ralph Abernathy across the bridge. I saw the same line of policemen and the same mob and I was scared. I even wanted to turn back, but my sister held my hand firm and in my heart I knew I was doing the right thing." [31]

"The Slap That Made Me a Man:

Rev. Fredrick Douglass Reese's Story"

Rev. Fredrick Douglass Reese is a living legend in the Civil Rights Movement, particularly in Selma, Alabama. Though his name may not be as well known as other luminaries in the movement, he was- and still is - a giant. A natural leader at an early age, he was 10, 11 and 12th grade class president at his high school. He was a person that most of his peers looked up to, but there was one incident that taught him a powerful lesson about strength and how to be a real man. It was a lesson that would influence his ideals about nonviolent resistance later on. One day at school, a 10 grade boy slapped him. Because he had a reputation for being well able to defend himself, all his peers knew what was about to happen to the foolhardy boy that slapped Fred. The boys formed a fight circle, and there in the middle of it stood Fred Reese and his opponent. But that day something came over him. He wasn't afraid of the other boy, he simply resisted the urge to fight and made a decision to handle things another way. He walked out of that circle and for the first time he went and reported the slap to the principal. Reese says he never forgot the incident and credits it for making him the man he is today. "The measure of a man or a woman is not determined by how much he gives but how much adversity he can take and still stand," he said. From that day on he was able to curb the urge he felt as a young man to "get back" at someone. He grew up to become a leader in the campaign for voter rights and marched with Dr. King in Selma on Bloody Sunday. His contributions to the movement for equality made him highly respected and his determination helped change the nation.

"I left Wilcox County after nine years of teaching to teach at R.B. Hudson High School in Dallas County. Hudson was the high school for black students and soon after I arrived there I was elected president of the Selma City Teachers Association, which was the all-black teachers association. I found out that there were many teachers with master degrees who were not registered to vote, so as president of teachers association I made that our priority. I believed our organization could take the lead in encouraging people to register to vote because teachers were looked upon

Dr. Reese marches across the Edmund Pettus with ,left to right, Corretta Scott King and John Lewis

Rev. Reese with Dr. Martin Luther King, Jr.

highly in the community and our influence might encourage other blacks to go register. I knew if I got them to go register, then others would follow.

In Dallas County at that time, blacks made up the largest population. Only 300 out of some 15,000 eligible blacks in Dallas County were registered to vote and I wanted to make sure we could get every eligible black voter registered. I contacted the Dallas County Voting League to engage them in holding a mass meeting that would hopefully get black citizens interested in going down to the county court house to file their application to become a registered voter.

During those days, the voter registration office was only open twice a month from 9 a.m. to Noon and 2 to 4 p.m. If you didn't get there during those hours then you had to wait until the next month to try to register. So what we did was to get as many blacks as we could to stand in line around the courthouse on the registration days because we wanted to send them a strong message that we were serious and we were interested in participating in the political process that would govern our lives.

People were standing in line all the way down Lauderdale Street and around Church Street to get into the courthouse and the board of registrar's office which was inside. Of course Jim Clark who was the sheriff at that time, would be outside on the steps to make sure that everybody was in line and to try to intimidate them.

Those who were able to get inside the courthouse stood in another line until a person from the registrar's office allowed them inside to fill out a registration form. The form was long and you had to indicate your name, address, and the name of a person who could verify that you actually lived at the address that was listed on the form.

A majority of the time, only about 25 blacks would even be called to go inside and be seen by the registrar to vote, and out of those 25, sometimes none of them would get to register because the registrar would provide some excuse to deny the registration. All this took place to discourage blacks and other minorities from voting.

On one occasion, Sheriff Clark pushed me down the steps of the courthouse with a Billy club while I was standing in line. He told us not to block the passage way and demanded to know why we were there. I told him we were there to register to vote and exercise our right as citizens.

106

The goal was to register to vote, but if they began arresting the teachers, that would spark attention and give our cause a lot of momentum and push the community to support our efforts. Plus, merchants knew the teachers supported many of their businesses. I remember Sheriff Clark saying, "If you're not off these steps I am going to arrest you and your marchers", but I said to myself that's exactly what I want you to do because by doing this we would be hurting the merchants where we shop.

My friend and fellow organizer A. J. Dirking, who had been my high school science teacher, was with me on the steps when Sheriff Clark began to push us down the steps.

I remember being punched in the side and while I was on the ground with Dirking, I saw his eyes become large in surprise. He was not used to violence like this. He looked up at me and asked me "What shall we do?" I answered, "We are going back!" To that response, his eyes became even larger! But, we went back a second time and were jabbed again.

By the third time, they still didn't arrest us. Clark made his move toward us and he was suddenly pulled inside the courthouse for about three minutes and whatever was discussed inside the court-house he came back out angrier and continued to jab and push us down the steps. Because we weren't being arrested, I led the marchers back to Brown Chapel Church. Soon afterward, when people saw the teachers march, then the beauticians and undertak-ers joined in. Soon more people in the community began taking a role in the demonstrations.

The next time around, when we stood in line at the courthouse, we were all given numbers to be waited on. It was small, but at least it was a sign of progress.

Ironically, while we were in Selma trying to encourage blacks to register to vote, Dr. King and his wife Coretta, a native of Marion, Alabama, were in Marion trying to organize blacks to vote there.

Soon after that, one of the SCLC workers, Rev. James Arms, was arrested in Marion and several members of the crowd brought us word that some of the whites were planning to kill him in the jail.

Many of us drove down to Marion and held a mass meeting. We marched to the jail where Arms was being held in hopes that our presence would stop them. Now as we were coming out of the church where the mass meeting was held, a state trooper shot out the street light and the street was completely dark. Pandemonium broke out and people began running everywhere. The state trooper and others began pursuing us with Billy clubs. Not far from the church was a little store and some people ran inside to get away of the madness.

Jimmy Lee Jackson was in that store and he ran out to protect his mother and grandfather who were being beaten by one of the troopers. The trooper shot him and his body was brought to a hospital in Selma where he died.

Jimmie Lee Jackson's death was the spark that ignited the voting rights march to Montgomery. When Jimmie Lee died people came to Selma from all over everywhere — all races and all denominations came together for the first time to unify in support of our right to vote.

On March 7, 1965, we attempted the first march from Selma to Montgomery, which was "Bloody Sunday." Dr. King was not here in Selma. He was in Atlanta. Dr. King came the following Monday after the terrible violence that took place on that bridge. People began to scatter and conditions were so chaotic, so we decided not to march to Montgomery until we got the go ahead from Dr. King.

They did what we called a 'turn-around' march. We simply walked to the end of the Edmund Pettus Bridge then; we turned around at the bridge. The ones that crossed the bridge the first time were ready to complete the march the second time, but this would be a symbolic march because we were waiting for a court order of protection to proceed.

People were coming into Selma from all over the country. When Judge Johnson issued the order of the court we decided to hold the march that Sunday. We marched on Sunday, Monday, and Tuesday and got to the outskirts of Montgomery. There was a flat bed truck with a stage, where entertainers like Harry Belafonte, Pearl Bailey and Sammy Davis Jr. performed for us.

The next day, we formed a line to march from St. Jude to the state capitol. I was on the front line. To my left was Hosea Williams; Dr. King and his wife Coretta; Dr. Ralph Bunch, the first African Nobel peace prize; Ralph Abernathy and his wife Juanita; John Lewis; A. Philip Randolph, who helped organize the 1963 March on Washington, and Rosa Parks.

That front line of the march moved all the way down Dexter Avenue to the Capitol steps to hear Dr. King speak. As I sat on that platform and looked out over that sea of humanity, a feeling of great triumphant after having gone through all the indignity and the violence, it now all seemed worth it. Soon after the march, President Lyndon B. Johnson signed into law the 1965 Voting Rights Act.

I sit here today thanking God that he had brought me through all of those trials, and tribulations. I claim no particular credit for what we accomplished, but I thank God for using me to achieve it and for the privilege of being a part of such a great movement. Now today, we have the first African-American president in Barak Obama, and it reminds me that our sacrifices were worth it." [32]

Chapter Nine

Still Shackled?

Growing up as an African-American in the South, I've always been aware of attitudes about race. All my life I have heard stories told by other African-Americans about what it meant to be Black in America. They are stories about struggle and pain; determination and triumph; and optimism about the future. They are stories that talk about the horrible atrocities black Americans endured and they are stories of amazing achievements in spite of the odds.

I'm only a generation or two from the civil rights movement myself, but I can distinctly remember the stories my grandmother told me about her life experiences. From slavery to sharecropping,the burden of life under Jim Crow, the constant fear of violence, to black resistance, political empowerment, and a renewed hope that eventually blossomed into a full scale social and political movement. Through it all, the hope and overwhelming desire for something better for the future remained.

Their struggles, like those of countless generations that came before them, have not been in vain. I've been fortunate to live to see the tremendous strides our country has made regarding race. Just think, it's been 400 years since slavery ended in this country and 50 years since the civil rights movement, yet the road to reconciliation has been rocky. I think of Emmett Till, four little girls in Birmingham, Bloody Sunday, the assassinations of JFK, MLK, RFK, the Rodney King beating, Hurricane Katrina, and the murder of Trayvon Martin.

Legislation now exists that ends discrimination in employment, housing, voting, public transportation and accommodations and public education. Through non-violent, civil disobedience, court battles and our voting power, we have righted many of the wrongs that have plagued our nation.

As a result, more African-Americans are attending colleges and universities. They lead industries, corporations and national organizations and hold more political offices on all levels — local, state and federal.

Moments after Barak Obama was elected as the first African-American president of the United States in 2008, I felt a sense of pride that is still hard to put into words. I could only image how such luminaries in the civil rights movement like Dr. Martin Luther King, Fannie Lou Hammer, Malcolm X, A. Phillip Randolph, Medgar Evers and others might feel, knowing that their sacrifices made Obama's historic election possible. I think they would be amazed by our progress as a nation in regards to race. They might also be glad to see those old shackles of intolerance finally fall away.

Yet, it's still clear that Black America's accomplishments and Obama's historic election haven't broken all the shackles we still grapple with.

For one, black infant mortality rates are more than twice that of whites, in a country that already has one of the highest infant mortality rates in the developed world. As black babies grow into toddlerhood and childhood the picture looks even more bleak. Two-thirds of black children live in single parent households, which is three times that of white children. And nearly 40 percent of black children under the age of five live at or below the poverty line. [33]

In school, black boys score lower on standardized tests, are nearly twice as likely to drop out of high school, three times as likely to be suspended or expelled from school and less likely to go on to a two-year or four-year college.

The unemployment rate is more than twice for minorities than it is for non-minorities, 16.7 and 8 percent respectively. [33]

How can we believe the shackles still don't remain when in our country the level of school segregation for Hispanics is the highest in the 40 years and segregation of blacks is back to levels not seen since the late 1960s? Or when the gaps in wealth, income, education and health care have widened over the last eight years? [34]

We are all Americans, but the pain of poverty is disproportionately cracking the backs of minorities. There are those who insist that the gap in wealth, income, health care and education is due to an inherent culture of victimization. If minorities only worked harder, they'd be fine, we are told. [34]

What can we do to break these shackles?

As a community we can begin by re-focusing on education. So many young people do not value an education because they just don't see its importance.

President Obama signed an executive order in July 2012 for an initiative to improve education for African Americans. The goals include: providing funding that will increase the percentage of black children who enter kindergarten, improving access to high-quality early learning and development programs; expanding access to high-level, rigorous course work and support services that will better prepare black students for college; recruiting highly qualified black teachers and principals; promoting a positive school climate that does not rely on methods that result in disparate use of disciplinary tools, and decreasing the disproportionate number of referrals to special education by addressing root causes of the referrals; and reducing the dropout rate of African-American students and increasing the proportion of African-American students who graduate from high school prepared for college and work.

This is a good first step, but change has to begin in our homes, too. Despite the economic and social shackles that have been broken, the African-American family is in trouble, too.

According to the U.S. Census Bureau's 2007, estimates nearly half of black Americans have never married—the highest percentage for all racial groups. Only 30 percent of blacks are now married.

Nearly 10 million black families lived in the United States in 2007.

Twenty-one percent of these families were married couples with children. This is the lowest for all racial groups. The U.S. average is 32.4 percent. Nearly one-third of these families were single mothers with children under 18. The U.S. average is 12.1 percent. A home headed by a single mom often equals an economically poor home. Slightly less than 20 percent of black families were grandparents raising their grandchildren. The U.S. average is 10 percent. [35]

We have to recommit to rebuilding our communities again by reducing the rate of fatherlessness and out-of-wedlock births. We must begin encouraging marriage, and protest policies that penalizing it by threatening to immediately cut off much needed financial assistance where there are two parents in the home. This and community building will help bring economic stability back to our neighborhoods.

We must advocate for policies that will keep our communities safe and work together to provide alternatives for our young people.

Finally we have to elect representatives who really care about our issues and are willing to fight for them, even if they are not politically popular.

I remember crying as Ma'dear told me the story about my great-grandma Rosanna's hands being burned by a white man because he saw her reading a book. She admonished me not to be sad and said, "No one can burn your hands for trying to learn now. Remember good does not exist without evil. Promise me that you will keep going in school as far as you can."

That promise kept me through many of life's challenges, and I believe that as a community and as a nation we need to keep our promise to our young people to leave our communities better off than when we inherited them.

I think we have come a long way in this country, but there is still work to do. Our accomplishments validate the sacrifices that my parents, their parents and generations before me made in order for us to enjoy the opportunities we have now.

Yes, some shackles still remain, but little by little, working together we will truly one day be free.

Sources

Chapter 1   Ole Rosanna

1. "Conditions of Antebellum Slavery 1830-1860". (n.d.). Retrieved 2012, from Public Broadcasting Service: http://www.pbs.org/wgbh/aia/part4/4p2956.html

Chapter 2   General Wilson and the Slave that Saved Marengo

2. "Conditions of Antebellum Slavery 1830-1860". (n.d.). Retrieved 2012, from Public Broadcasting Service: http://www.pbs.org/wgbh/aia/part4/4p2956.html

3. Most Haunted Places in America. (2010, February 26). Retrieved April 2012, from Haunts of Marengo: www.ghosteyes.com/haunts-marengo

4. Society, L. H. (1979). Lowndesboro's Picturesque Legacies. Lowndesboro: Lowndesboro Heritage Society. First Edition.

Chapter 3   Confronting Power: Breaking Shackles Through Black Resistance

5. Slaughter, T. P. (1991). Bloody Dawn: The Christiana Riot and Racial Violence in the Antebellum North. New York: Oxford University Press.

Chapter 4   Miles and Miles of Drought

6. Cuordileone, K. (n.d.). The Meaning of Emancipation in the Reconstruction Era. Retrieved May 2012, from Investigation U.S. History: http://investigationhistory.ashp.cuny.edu/m6.html

7. Wormser, R. (2012). The Rise and Fall of Jim Crow. Retrieved May 2012, from PBS.org: www.pbs.org/wnet/jim-crow/stories_events_reconstruct.html

8. African-American Odysseys: "Reconstruction and Its Aftermath" . (2008, March). Retrieved May 2012, from The Library of Congress: American Memory: www.memory.loc.gov/ammen/aaohtml/exhibit/aopart5.html

9. Katzman, D. M. (2012). Black Migration. Retrieved April 2012, from Answers: http://www.answers.com/topic/black-migration

10. W.E.B. Du Bois, "The Talented Tenth," from *The Negro Problem: A Series of Articles by Representative Negroes of To-day* (New York, 1903).

11. WBGH-Public Television. (2002). Reconstruction and Black Education. Retrieved April 2012, from Teacher's Domain: www.teachersdomain.org/resource/osi04.soc.ush.civil.reconstruction

    Booker T. & W.E.B. Two Nations of Black America http://www.pbs.org/wgbh/pages/frontline/shows/

Chapter 5 Hanging Mothers

12. American Experience. (2012). Retrieved 2012, from PBS.org: http://www.pbs.org/wgbh/amex/till/peopleevents/e_lynch.html

13. Eastern Digital Resources. (1998). The South Carolina Secessionist: Sherman's March through South Carolina. Retrieved March 2012, from The Civil War in South Carolina: Eastern Digital Resources: www.researchonline.net/sccw/scsec006.htm

14. Hanging of Amy Spain. (1865, September 30). Retrieved from Harper's Weekly: www.blackhistory.harpweek.com

15. Without Sanctuary. (n.d.). Retrieved from http://withoutsanctuary.org/pics_34_text.html

16. Myers, Christopher (2006). "Killing Them by the Wholesale: A Lynching Rampage in South Georgia" pgs. 214-235 in Georgia Historical Quarterly. Vol. XC. No. 2. Summer 2006.

17. In E. H. Kevern J. Verney. "Maggie Howze and Alma Howze " Thirty Years of Lynching in the United States, 1889–1918. http://myloc.gov/Exhibitions/naacp/earlyyears. New York : NAACP Collection, Manuscript Division, Library of Congress (045.00.00)

18. Strange Fruit. (n.d.). Retrieved May 2012, from http://www. strangefruit.org/nelson.htm.

19. They Lynching Calendar. http://www.autopsis.org/foot/lynch-places1.html (accessed May 22,2012, 2012).

Chapter 6   Remembering Rosewood

20. The Real Rosewood Foundation, Inc. P O Box 252 Archer, Florida 32618 http://www.rosewoodflorida.com/history.html

21. Jan. 20, 2012 interview of Mary Hall Daniels Samuel Proctor Oral History Program, University of Florida by Ryan Morini with Sherry DuPree

22. Sarasota Herald-tribune Feb. 17, 1997 Rosewood Violence Depicted in Movie- Associated Press

23. Black Past.org http://www.blackpast.org/?q=aah/rosewood-massacre-1923An Online Reference Guide to African American History by Quintard Taylor, Scott and Dorothy Bullitt Professor of American History University of Washington, Seatt

Chapter 7   Sick and Tired

24. Dubriwny, K. P. (n.d.). University of Texas A&M College of Liberal Arts. "Fannie Lou Hamer's Testimony to Credentials Committee, DNC" (1964) http://liberalarts.tamu.edu/html/spot-influential-civil-rights-speeches-hamer.html

25. Shuttlesworth, Fred. (2012, June 7). Retrieved from Wikipedia.org: http://en.wikipedia.org/wiki/Fred_Shuttlesworth

26. Arsenault, R. (2006). Freedom Riders:1961 and the Struggle for Racial Justice. In R. Arsenault, Freedom Riders:1961 and the struggle for racial justice (p. 106). Oxford University Press.

27. Manis, A. (Summer-Fall 2000). Birmingham's Reverend Fred Shuttlesworth: Unsung Hero of the Civil Rights Movement".

Baptist History and Heritage.

28. McWhorter, D. (2001). Carry Me Home: Birmingham, Alabama, the Climactic Battle of the Civil Rights revolution. New York: Simon and Schuster.

29. Gates, V. (2011, October 5). "Birmingham Civil Rights Leader Fred Shuttlesworth Dies". Reuters .

30. Shuttlesworth, Sephia. (2013, February). T. Watkins, Interviewer

30a. Photo: *Huff Post Black Voices. http://www.huffington post.com /2013/02/23/civil-rights-sit-ins-black-history-photo_n_2748918.html*

Chapter 8   Stories from Selma

31. Bland, J. (2012, May). "Through the Eyes of the Child". (T. Watkins, Interviewer)

32. Reese, R. F. (2012, June). "The Slap That Made Me a Man: The Story of Rev. Fredrick Douglas Reese". (T. Watkins, Interviewer)

Chapter 9   Still Shackled?

33. Young, L. (2011, December 5). Still Waiting: Black Male Achievement in America. Retrieved July 2012, from Huffington Post Black Voices: http://www.huffingtonpost.com/lavar-young/black-male-achievement_b_1121379.html

34. McKissack, F. (2008, November). The Progressive. Retrieved July 28, 2012, from Progressive.org: http://www.progressive.org/mp/mckissack110508.html

35. Bowman, B. (2010). http://www.theroot.com/views/poor-state-black-families. Retrieved July 31, 2012, from The Root: http://www.theroot.com/views/poor-state-black-families